# AQA PSYCHOLOGY A LEVEL YEAR 2. TWO A STAR EXAMS. PAPER 1 (TWO SETS).

*Full mark answers to 2 Past Papers.*

By Joseph Anthony Campbell

# CONTENTS

# AUTHOR'S NOTE.

This book will provide you with crystal clear and accurate examples of 'A' star grade AQA A level Psychology paper 1 examinations from the new syllabus and enables students to achieve the same grade in their upcoming examinations.

I teach both GCSE and A level Psychology and I am a qualified and experienced Psychology teacher and tutor of over 17 years standing. I teach, write and provide independent tuition in Central and West London.

The resources in this book WILL help you get an A or A star in your AQA A level Psychology examinations, as they have done and will continue to do so, for my students.

Best wishes,

Joseph

# ABOUT THE AUTHOR.

I graduated from the Universities of Liverpool and Leeds and I obtained first class honours in my teacher training.

I have taught and provided private tuition for over 17 years up to University level. I also write academic resources for the Times Educational Supplement.

My tuition students have been fortunate enough to attain places to study at Oxford, Cambridge and Imperial College, London and other Russell Group Universities. The students have done very well in their examinations and one Psychology student even obtained full UMS marks in her A2 Psychology examination. I hope and know that my Psychology books can enable you to take the next step on your academic journey.

# SUMMARY OF THE EXAMINATION PAPERS.

The examinations are linear i.e., they are all done at the end of each year.

There are **2** examination papers for Psychology AS level.

There are **3** examination papers for Psychology A level.

(I have written further books to help you with the AS level examinations and Paper 2 and Paper 3 of the A level and I have provided details of the AS level Psychology papers and the Paper 2 and Paper 3 A level topics in those Psychology books).

In this book, we are concerned with Paper 1 of the A level examinations which is completed at the end of your 'A' levels (usually the end of Year 2).

Paper **1** is divided into **4** sections:

Section A – Social Influence

Section B – Memory

Section C – Attachment

Section D - Psychopathology

Each section is worth 24 marks and the paper has a total of 96 marks.
There is 2 hours (120 minutes) for the exam (unless you have extra time).

Each A level Paper is worth one third of your total A level Psychology mark.

The exam structure is complicated. In each section there will be multiple choice questions, short answer questions and at least one extended writing question. This is why the examples in this book are particularly useful as you will need to familiarise yourself with these types of questions and their structure for each examination. They range from 1 to 16 marks per question.

By Joseph Anthony Campbell

# AQA A-LEVEL PSYCHOLOGY (7182/1)
# PAPER 1
# INTRODUCTORY TOPICS IN PSYCHOLOGY.
# SPECIMEN MATERIAL (FIRST SET) 2017

# SECTION A: SOCIAL INFLUENCE

*Answer **all** questions in this section (24 marks and 30 minutes for each section on Paper 1)*

*0 1 Which of the following terms best matches the statements below? Choose **one** term that matches **each** statement and write A, B, C, D or E in the box next to it. Use each letter once only.*

*A Identification*
*B Informational social influence*
*C Normative social influence*
*D Compliance*
*E Internalisation*

**[4 marks] (5 minutes) (AO1 = 4)**

*Publicly changing behaviour whilst maintaining a different private view. [1 mark]*

D

*Group pressure leading to a desire to fit in with the group. [1 mark]*

C

*When a person lacks knowledge of how to behave and looks to the group for guidance. [1 mark]*

B

*Conforming to the behaviour of a role model. [1 mark]*

A

*0 2 Briefly outline __and__ evaluate the findings of any __one__ study of social influence.*

**[4 marks] (5 minutes) (AO1 = 2; AO3 = 2) (100 words maximum)**

Asch placed male participants in an unambiguous situation where the majority of participants conformed at least once when confederates gave the same wrong answer to a question comparing line lengths across various trials. 75% of participants conformed at least once across 18 trials.

(AO1=2)

The study lacks ecological validity however, as whether the participants were right or wrong did not really matter to the participants; they may have been less likely to conform if their answers had real–life consequences. Also, in terms of ethics, the participants were deceived as to the true nature of the study.

(AO3=2)

**(95 words)**

*0 3 Read the item and then answer the question that follows.*

*Two psychology students were discussing the topic of social influence.*

*'I find it fascinating how some people are able to resist social influence', said Jack. 'It must be the result of having a confident personality.'*

*'I disagree', replied Sarah. 'I think resisting social influence depends much more on the presence of others.'*

*Discuss two explanations of resistance to social influence. As part of your discussion, refer to the views expressed by Jack and Sarah in the conversation above.*

**[16 marks] (20 minutes) (AO1 = 6; AO2 = 4; AO3 = 6) (400 words maximum)**

One explanation of resistance to social influence is that of social support, a situational factor. Sarah states that resistance depends on 'the presence of others' and Milgram found that participants are less likely to obey authority if there were other dissenting confederates present. Asch found similar results in variations of his experiment on conformity in an unambiguous situation when he tested the effect of the participant having a supporter in the group i.e., one of the confederates agreed with the participant. Having a fellow dissenter who disagreed with the majority broke the unanimity of the group. This made it easier for the participant to resist the pressure to conform and the rate of conformity fell to 5.5%. This finding is reflected in Sarah's comment that 'social influence depends much more on the presence of others.'

Jack however suggests that dispositional factors in resisting social influence are more important. Another explanation of resistance is that of 'locus of control'. Jack states that '...how some people are able to resist social influence...must be the result of having a confident personality'. If someone has an internal locus of control, they are more likely to accept personal responsibility for their own actions. They are therefore less likely to obey authoritative demands that are against both their morals and views. If someone has an external locus of control, they are less likely to accept personal responsibility for their actions and are therefore more likely to feel helpless and obedient when confronted with a perceived authority figure. This explanation of resistance to social influence provides an alternative, viable explanation through a dispositional factor as to why people would resist social influence.

However as to the psychological experiments that have provided these two explanations of resistance to social influence, both Asch and Milgram's experiments have been criticised for the deceptive elements of their studies. Asch and Milgram' participants encounter the ethical issue of deception as Asch's participants believed that they were taking part in a study to determine line lengths whilst Milgram's participants believed that the experiment was based on the effects of punishment on learning and that they were actually providing electric shocks to participants. The experiments could have had a long-term impact on the participants and both experiments could therefore lack validity and be criticised for their levels of ecological validity due to the fact that they were both artificial laboratory experiments.

**(397 words)**

# SECTION B: MEMORY

*Answer <u>all</u> questions in this section (24 marks and 30 minutes for each section on Paper 1)*

*Read the item and then answer the questions that follow.*

*An experiment was carried out to test the effects of learning similar and dissimilar information on participants' ability to remember.*

*In <u>Stage 1</u> of the experiment, 10 participants in <u>Group A</u>, the 'similar' condition, were given a list of 20 place names in the UK. They were given two minutes to learn the list. 10 different participants in <u>Group B</u>, the 'dissimilar' condition, were given the same list of 20 place names in the UK. They were also given two minutes to learn the list.*

*In <u>Stage 2</u> of the experiment, participants in <u>Group A</u> were given a different list of 20 more place names in the UK, and were given a further two minutes to learn it. Participants in <u>Group B</u> were given a list of 20 boys' names, and were given a further two minutes to learn it.*

*In <u>Stage 3</u> of the experiment, all participants were given five minutes to recall as many of the 20 place names in the UK, from the list in <u>Stage 1</u>, as they could. The raw data from the two groups is below.*

*Table 1: Number of place names recalled from the list in Stage 1.*

| Group A | Group B |
|---------|---------|
| 5 | 11 |
| 6 | 10 |
| 4 | 11 |
| 7 | 13 |
| 8 | 12 |
| 4 | 14 |
| 5 | 15 |
| 4 | 11 |
| 6 | 14 |
| 7 | 14 |

*0 4-0 1 What is the most appropriate measure of central tendency for calculating the average of the scores, from Table 1, in each of the two groups? Justify your answer.*

**[2 marks] (2.5 minutes) (AO2 = 2) (50 words maximum)**

The mean is the appropriate measure of central tendency for calculating the average of the scores. The mean is the most sensitive method as it takes all the scores in each data set into account.

**(35 words)**

*0 4-0 2 Calculate the measure of central tendency you have identified in your answer to question 04.0 1 for Group A and Group B. Show your calculations for each group.*

**[4 marks] (5 minutes) (AO2 = 4)**

5+6+4+7+8+4+5+4+6+7=56/10= 5.6 = Group A mean

11+10+11+13+12+14+15+11+14+14=125/10= 12.5 =Group B mean

*0 4-0 3 In <u>Stage 3</u> of the experiment, several participants in <u>Group A</u>, the 'similar'
condition, recalled words from the <u>Stage 2</u> list rather than the <u>Stage 1</u> list.*

*Use your knowledge of forgetting to explain why this may have occurred.*

**[2 marks] (2.5 minutes) (AO2 = 2) (50 words maximum)**

The information presented in Stage 1 and Stage 2 was similar and the new information
disrupted/interfered with the recall of previous information. This is called retroactive
interference.

**(27 words)**

*0 5 Describe <u>and</u> evaluate the working memory model of memory.*

**[16 marks] (20 minutes) (AO1 = 6; AO3 = 10) (400 words maximum)**

The working memory model (WMM) was created by Baddeley and Hitch in 1974 and
the model proposed that short term memory was comprised of three different stores;
the phonological loop, the episodic buffer and the visuo-spatial sketchpad. The central
executive receives all of the information that is paid attention to (attentional focus)
and directs the information to one of the three slave systems according to its type.
Speech-based information is directed to the phonological loop; visual and spatial
information is directed towards the visuo-spatial sketchpad and the episodic buffer
(2000) stores information from the other two slave systems and integrates the
information together to form episodes along with information from long term
memory (LTM) in order to make complete scenes or form 'episodes. All of the slave
systems have limited capacity and duration and therefore in order to store
information for a long time, information must be passed on to the long-term
memory.

The working memory model is supported by evidence such as the case study of KF by Shallice and Washington (1974). KF sustained brain damage in a motorbike accident and had problems with certain areas of short-term memory. KF could recall and process visual information but had trouble recalling words verbally. This suggests that he had an impaired articulatory loop but an intact visuo-spatial sketchpad. KF's condition could not be explained by the multi-store model of memory (MSM) which delineates short term memory as one store and in the case of KF it instead supports the working memory model's theory that short-term memory is made up of multiple stores and an active processor unlike the multi-store model of memory which contains a discrete store only.

The working memory model also does not place as much emphasis on rehearsal as the multi-store model. Rehearsal is only one possible process in the working memory model which helps to explain how information enters the long-term memory after little or no rehearsal. This means that the working memory model allows for other explanations on processes rather than one finite explanation as provided by the multi-store model.

However, some psychologists argue that the central executive is too vague and simplistic in its description; it is merely described as 'attention' in the working memory model. The central executive concept is also not supported as it is extremely difficult to design tasks to test it and therefore there is little empirical evidence for its existence.

**(400 words)**

# SECTION C: ATTACHMENT

*Answer __all__ questions in this section (24 marks and 30 minutes for each section on Paper 1)*

*06 Name __three__ stages in the development of attachments identified by Schaffer.*

**[3 marks] (3.75 minutes) (AO1 = 3)**

1 Pre-attachment (Asocial)
2 Indiscriminate (Multiple)
3 Discriminate (Single)

*07 Read the item and then answer the question that follows.*

*A nursery school worker and her manager were chatting at the end of the day.*

*'How did the new toddlers settle in today?' asked the manager.*

*'They behaved very differently', replied the nursery school worker. 'Max was distressed when his mother left but was happy to see her at the end of the day.'*

*'Jessica arrived clinging to her mother and I could not calm her down when her mother left.'*

*'William barely seemed to notice when his mother left and did not even look up when she returned to collect him.'*

*Name the attachment type demonstrated by <u>each</u> of the children in the conversation above by writing the attachment type next to the name below.*

**[3 marks] (3.75 minutes) (AO2 = 3)**

| | |
|---|---|
| *Max* | Secure |
| *Jessica* | Insecure – resistant |
| *William* | Insecure – avoidant |

*0 8 Briefly evaluate learning theory as an explanation of attachment.*

**[4 marks] (5 minutes) (AO3 = 4) (100 words maximum)**

Support for learning theory is derived from scientific research involving research on animals. This is a limitation because it presents the problem of anthropomorphic extrapolation because it is not possible to fully extrapolate from animals to humans as humans and animals are inherently different. It is also difficult to tell in learning theory if an association has taken place and if it ever will take place when studying babies in their early months. For example, Schaffer and Emerson (1964) found that many babies did not have their mother as the primary attachment figure despite the mother being the primary caregiver.

**(100 words)**

*0 9 Read the item and then answer the question that follows.*

*A group of researchers used 'event sampling' to observe children's friendships over a period of three weeks at break times and lunchtimes during the school day.*

*Explain what is meant by 'event sampling'.*

**[2 marks] (2.5 minutes) (AO1 = 2) (50 words maximum)**

'Event sampling' is when researchers comprise a list of events they want to study (e.g., holding hands, speaking aloud) and compile a period of time in which to record said events (e.g., 5 hourly periods). The researchers then record the events that occur in the period of time previously designated.

**(50 words)**

*1 0 The investigation in <u>question 09</u> is an example of a 'naturalistic observation'. Briefly discuss how observational research might be improved by conducting observations in a controlled environment.*

**[4 marks] (5 minutes) (AO3 = 4) (100 words maximum)**

Controlled environments such as laboratory experiments offer a strong level of control of extraneous variables during observational research. Extraneous variables can interfere or affect the results of the observational research. The removal or minimising of said extraneous variables makes it easier to both establish a causal relationship between the independent and dependent variable and for a later researcher to conduct the same experiment/observation and replicate the same results. This increases both the reliability and the validity of the observational research which could be improved by conducting observations in a controlled environment.

**(91 words)**

*11 Discuss research into the influence of early attachment on adult relationships.*

**[8 marks] (10 minutes) (AO1 = 4; AO3 = 4) (200 words maximum)**

Hazan and Shaver (1987) conducted a 'love quiz' in a local newspaper. The quiz assessed the attachment type (secure, insecure resistant or insecure avoidant) between participants and their parents. The other section assessed their current beliefs about romantic love. The first 620 responses were analysed and secure children tended to have fully functional, trusting relationships; insecure resistant children were more likely to be extremely worried that they were not loved in their relationships and insecure avoidant children tended to fear intimacy. This provides support for Bowlby's theory that adult relationships are influenced by early attachment.

However, Freud and Dann (1951) provided evidence that those early attachments may not have as large an effect on adult relationships as Hazan and Shaver's (1987) results implied. They studied 6 children who were orphaned during World War Two and raised in a deportation camp. They were unable to form any adult attachments. However, when the children grew up, they developed average intelligence and were able to form fully functioning relationships. Freud and Dann concluded that this was because they had formed attachments amongst themselves as children. This offers an alternative interpretation of a viable early attachment and its influence on later adult relationships.

**(199 words)**

# SECTION D: PSYCHOPATHOLOGY

*Answer __all__ questions in this section (24 marks and 30 minutes for each section on Paper 1)*

*1 2 Which __two__ of the following are examples of Jahoda's criteria for 'ideal mental health'? Shade __two__ boxes only. For each answer completely fill in the circle alongside the appropriate answer.*

**[2 marks] (2.5 minutes) (AO1 = 2)**

*A Dependence on others*
*B Environmental mastery* SHADE THIS BOX
*C Lack of inhibition*
*D Maladaptiveness*
*E Resistance to stress* SHADE THIS BOX

*1 3 Read the item and then answer the question that follows.*

*The following article appeared in a magazine:*

*Hoarding disorder – A 'new' mental illness*

*Most of us are able to throw away the things we don't need on a daily basis. Approximately 1 in 1000 people, however, suffer from hoarding disorder, defined as 'a difficulty parting with items and possessions, which leads to severe anxiety and extreme clutter that affects living or work spaces'.*

*Apart from 'deviation from ideal mental health', outline <u>three</u> definitions of abnormality. Refer to the article above in your answer.*

**[6 marks] (7.5 minutes) (AO1 = 3; AO2 = 3) (150 words maximum)**

One definition of abnormality is a deviation from statistical norms. Behaviour that is rare statistically is considered abnormal within this approach (people on the tail ends of a bell curve graph are statistically rare and therefore abnormal). People with 'hoarding disorder' are '1 in 1000 people', they are therefore statistically rare and abnormal.

Another definition of abnormality is an individual being unable to function adequately. Criteria for diagnosis include dysfunctional behaviour (behaviour which contrasts with the cultures accepted and expected behaviour) and personal distress (the individual is excessively emotional). In this case, the 'hoarding disorder' is causing the sufferers, 'severe anxiety'.

Deviation from social norms is a third definition of abnormality. This outlines an individual who contrasts with the expected and accepted behaviours of their society (the social norms). As the article states 'Most of us are able to throw away the things we don't need on a daily basis'.

**(150 words)**

*1 4 Read the item and then answer the question that follows.*

*Kirsty is in her twenties and has had a phobia of balloons since one burst near her face when she was a little girl. Loud noises such as 'banging' and 'popping' cause Kirsty extreme anxiety, and she avoids situations such as birthday parties and weddings, where there might be balloons.*

*Suggest how the behavioural approach might be used to explain Kirsty's phobia of balloons.*

**[4 marks] (5 minutes) (AO2 = 4) (100 words maximum)**

The behavioural approach may explain Kirsty's phobia of balloons as a product of classical conditioning i.e., Kirsty has learnt to associate balloons with fear. This means that a neutral stimulus (NS) (a balloon) has been presented with an unconditioned stimulus (UCS-loud noise) and produced an unconditioned response (UCR-fear). In this way balloons inspire and cause a response of fear in Kirsty. This fear has been maintained through operant conditioning as Kirsty's avoidance of situations where there might be balloons has prevented this conditioned anxiety and fear (CR-fear) from occurring (negative reinforcement). Thus, she may continually repeat this avoidant behaviour.

**(99 words)**

*1 5 Read the item and then answer the questions that follow.*

*Twenty depressed patients were treated using cognitive behavioural therapy. Over the course of the six-week treatment, each patient's mood was monitored every week using a self-report mood scale (where a score of 20 = extremely positive mood and a score of 0 = extremely negative mood). Each week they also completed a quality of sleep questionnaire which was scored from 10 = excellent sleep to 0 = very poor sleep.*

*At the end of the study the researchers correlated each patient's final mood score with his or her final sleep score.*

*1 5-0 2 Outline <u>one</u> way in which the researchers should have dealt with ethical issues in this study.*

**[2 marks] (2.5 minutes) (AO3 = 2) (50 words maximum)**

The researchers should have constantly offered or made the participants aware of the right for them to withdraw from the study. This would prevent participant discomfort and distress.

**(28 words)**

*1 5-0 3 The sleep questionnaire used by the researchers had not been checked to see whether or not it was a reliable measure of sleep quality.*

*Explain how this study could be modified by checking the sleep questionnaire for test-retest reliability.*

**[4 marks] (5 minutes) (AO3 = 4) (100 words maximum)**

This would be achieved by modifying the sleep questionnaire for test-retest reliability. Firstly, the participants would complete the sleep questionnaire more than once. The scores would then be correlated from each questionnaire. A scatter graph would also be used and on one axis the first tests results and, on another axis, the later test's results. This would then be assessed using a Spearman's Rho test and the reliability is then determined by comparing the correlation with the statistical table. It would be expected to display a strong, positive correlation between the two sets of scores.

**(95 words)**

*1 6 Outline cognitive behaviour therapy as a treatment for depression.*

**[4 marks] (5 minutes) (AO1 = 4) (100 words maximum)**

Cognitive behavioural therapy (CBT) attempts to identify and rectify the patient's faulty cognitions. There are many ways that the therapist and patient can do this. The therapist tries to help the client discern that these cognitions are faulty by questioning them and focusing upon the clients' successes in life. The client may be encouraged to keep a diary to help them become more aware of their thoughts and feelings. The therapy aims to mostly focus on what the client's personal situation is but the therapist may also draw on the client's past experiences.

**(93 words)**

# AQA A–LEVEL PSYCHOLOGY (7182/1)

# PAPER 1

# INTRODUCTORY TOPICS IN PSYCHOLOGY.

## 2017 (SECOND SET)

## WEDNESDAY 7 JUNE 2017

## AFTERNOON

## TIME ALLOWED: 2 HOURS

# SECTION A: SOCIAL INFLUENCE

*Answer __all__ questions in this section (24 marks and 30 minutes for each section on Paper 1)*

*In an experiment, researchers arranged for participants to complete a very personal and embarrassing questionnaire in a room with other people. Each participant was tested individually. The other people were confederates of the experimenter.*

*In condition 1: the confederates completed the questionnaire.*

*In condition 2: the confederates refused to complete the questionnaire and asked to leave the experiment.*

*The researchers tested 15 participants in condition 1, and 15 different participants in condition 2.*

*The researchers recorded the number of participants who completed the questionnaire in each condition.*

*0 1 Identify the type of data in this experiment. Explain your answer.*

**[2 marks] (2.5 minutes) (AO2 = 2) (50 words maximum)**

The type of data in this experiment is quantitative data. This is because the researchers counted the number of participants who completed the questionnaire in each condition i.e., conditions one and two and the data is numerical.

**(37 words)**

*0 2 Using your knowledge of social influence, explain the likely outcome of this experiment.*

**[3 marks] (3.75 minutes) (AO2 = 3) (75 words maximum)**

It is likely that more participants will complete the questionnaire in condition one than in condition two.

In condition one, the naive participant is likely to conform to the majority through normative social influence as the other confederates (the majority) completed the questionnaire.

However, the participants in condition two would be less likely to conform (and complete the questionnaire) as they have an ally (social support) of disobedient role models who support a non-conformist view.

**(75 words)**

*For this study, the researchers had to use different participants in each condition and this could have affected the results.*

*0 3 Outline __one__ way in which the researchers could have addressed this issue.*

**[4 marks] (5 minutes) (AO3 = 4) (100 words maximum)**

Firstly, the psychologist must randomly allocate participants to each condition by writing down all the names of the participants on slips of paper and then put them in a hat. Then the psychologist must randomly withdraw 15 names and put them in condition 1 and then withdraw another 15 names and put them in condition 2. These will be the participants in condition 1 and condition 2 and should thus adequately address the issue above.

**(75 words)**

*In order to analyse the difference in the number of participants who completed the questionnaire in each condition, the researchers used a chi-squared test.*

*0 4 Apart from reference to the level of measurement, give __two__ reasons why the researchers used the chi-squared test.*

**[2 marks] (2.5 minutes) (AO2 = 2) (50 words maximum)**

The Chi-Squared test is suitable because the design is of independent groups with independent data – i.e., they were in either group 1 or group 2.

Furthermore, the Chi-Squared test is also suitable when researchers are looking for a difference or an association between two variables.

**(45 words)**

*The calculated value of chi-squared in the experiment described on page 2 is __3.97__*

*Table 1: Critical values for the chi-squared test*

*Level of significance*
*df 0.1   0.05   0.02   0.01*
*1 2.71   3.84   5.41   6.64*

*The calculated value of chi-squared should be equal to or greater than the critical value to be statistically significant.*

*0 5 With reference to the critical values in __Table 1__, explain whether or not the calculated value of chi-squared is significant at the 5% level.*

**[2 marks] (2.5 minutes) (AO2 = 2) (50 words maximum)**

The value of chi-squared is significant at the 5% level as the calculated (observed) value (3.97) is more than the critical table value of 3.84 at the 5% level.

**(29 words)**

*0 6 Discuss the authoritarian personality as an explanation for obedience.*

**[8 marks] (10 minutes) (AO1 = 3; AO3 = 5) (200 words maximum)**

An authoritarian personality is a collection of traits developed from overly strict parenting. An authoritarian personality is more likely to be conformist and obey and be servile towards people of perceived higher status and to be hostile towards those of perceived lower status. Adorno et al (1950) conducted a study of over 2000 participants using a questionnaire called the F-scale. This measured fascist tendencies, which is potentially at the core of the authoritarian personality.

(AO1 = 3)

Those with an authoritarian personality are generally more uncomfortable with uncertainty, and view everything as being either right or wrong, thus, demonstrating an inflexible attitude. There is also research support for the authoritarian personality as an explanation for obedience. Milgram (1963) found, when aiming to discern if there was a link between high levels of obedience and an authoritarian personality, that participants who were fully obedient in his study, scored higher on the F-scale in comparison to the disobedient participants. However, it is difficult to establish cause and effect between overly strict parenting and later levels of obedience. It is also difficult to easily account for obedience of entire social groups/societies. Furthermore, there may be individual differences that contribute to the development of the authoritarian personality.

(AO3 = 5)

**(200 words)**

*0 7 Outline one alternative explanation for obedience.*

**[3 marks] (3.75 minutes) (AO1 = 3) (75 words maximum)**

An alternative explanation for obedience is the agentic shift/state explanation. When a person acts independently this is called an autonomous state. The opposite of this is an agentic state, which occurs when an individual carries out the orders of an authority figure without thinking, with reduced moral accountability for their actions. To shift from autonomy to 'agency' is referred to as the 'agentic shift' and this is when a person experiences a diffusion of responsibility.

**(75 words)**

# SECTION B: MEMORY

*Answer __all__ questions in this section (24 marks and 30 minutes for each section on Paper 1)*

*Two types of long-term memory are procedural memory and episodic memory.*

*0 8 Explain __two__ differences between procedural memory and episodic memory.*

**[4 marks] (5 minutes) (AO3 = 4) (100 words maximum)**

One difference between procedural memory and episodic memory is that procedural memories of actions, motor skills etc. have become 'automatic' and are unavailable for conscious inspection and difficult to explain verbally i.e., non-declarative. Whereas episodic memories, which include memories of personal experiences, can be expressed verbally i.e., they are declarative.

Another difference between procedural memory and episodic memory is that each type of memory may reside in a different area of the brain. Episodic memories are associated with the hippocampus whereas procedural memories are associated with the motor cortex. Procedural memories may also be more resistant to forgetting or amnesia.

**(100 words)**

*In an investigation into memory, participants were presented with two different lists of words.*

*List A: Flip    Flit  Flop  Flap  Flab  Flan   Flat*
*List B: Huge Large Great Giant Vast Mighty Epic*

*After seeing the lists, participants were tested on their ability to recall the words.*

*When tested immediately, participants found it more difficult to recall the words from List A in the correct order.*

*When tested after 30 minutes, participants found it more difficult to recall the words from List B in the correct order.*

*0 9 Using your knowledge of coding in memory, explain these findings.*

**[4 marks] (5 minutes) (AO2 = 4) (100 words maximum)**

Immediate task – list A is made up of words that are acoustically similar and this will cause confusion (when tested immediately) as short-term memory (STM) uses acoustic, sound-based coding. This explains why participants found it difficult to recall the words in List A immediately after the presentation.

Delayed task – list B is made up of words that are semantically similar and this will cause confusion (when tested after 30 minutes) as recall in long-term memory (LTM) uses semantic, meaning-based coding. This explains why participants found it difficult to recall the words in List B after 30 minutes.

**(99 words)**

*1 0 Outline and evaluate research (theories and/or studies) into the effects of misleading information on eyewitness testimony.*

**[16 marks] (20 minutes) (AO1=6; AO3 = 10) (400 words maximum)**

Loftus and Palmer conducted studies into eyewitness testimony in 1974. They played a video of a car crash to participants and asked them 'how fast was the car going when it...the other car'. In different conditions they found that if they used the word 'smashed' the participants estimated an average speed of 41 miles per hour compared to an average estimation of 32 miles per hour if they used the word 'contacted'. A week later they also asked 'Did you see any broken glass?' using the word 'smashed' for one group, 'hit' for another and a third control group had no indication of speed given to them. The 'smashed' group had a higher number reporting 'broken glass', even though there was none.

(AO1 = 4)

In evaluating, we are aware that viewing a car crash on video is not as emotionally stimulating and produces less adrenaline than being in a real car crash and this may affect the results as it is also less ecologically valid. This demonstrates experimental reductionism also as the complex process of memory is reduced to the effect of the wording of a leading question on eyewitness memory. Therefore, their results do not reflect actual car accidents and we are unable to conclude if the effect of leading questions is ecologically valid in this context. The participants may have also guessed the aims of the experiment and thus displayed demand characteristics. However, both experiments also show that leading questions may have a long-term effect on eyewitness testimony.

(AO3 =5)

Gabbert et al. (2003) investigated the effect of post-event discussion. Her participants watched a video of a girl stealing money. Participants in the co-witness group were told that they had watched the same video; however, they had seen different perspectives.

(AO1 = 2)

In evaluating, 71% of the witnesses in the co-witness group recalled information they had not seen, despite the fact that they had not seen her commit a crime. This could be the result of poor memory, where people assimilate new information into personalised accounts of the event and are unable to distinguish between what they have seen and what they have heard. However, paired discussions could have clearly influenced the recall of crime and co-witnesses mixing may have led to misinformation, memory contamination and memory conformity. Witnesses may have clearly conformed with others to receive social approval.

Further research is required to demonstrate the exact effects of misleading information on eyewitness testimony.

(AO3 = 5)


**(400 words)**

# SECTION C: ATTACHMENT

*Answer <u>all</u> questions in this section (24 marks and 30 minutes for each section on Paper 1)*

*Answer <u>all</u> questions in this section*

*1 1 Which <u>two</u> of the following are associated with an insecure-resistant attachment type? Choose <u>two</u> from the options <u>A, B, C, D</u> and <u>E.</u>*

[2 marks] (2.5 minutes) (AO1 = 2)

*A Extreme stranger anxiety*
*B Indifference when the mother leaves the room*
*C Low willingness to explore the new environment*
*D Moderate levels of separation anxiety*
*E Obvious joy when reunited with the mother*

A

C

*1 2 Name <u>three</u> of the stages of attachment identified by Schaffer.*

[3 marks] (3.75 minutes) (AO1 = 3)

Pre-Attachment (asocial)

Indiscriminate (diffuse)

Discriminate (specific)


*13 What is meant by 'reciprocity' in the context of caregiver-infant interaction?*

**[2 marks] (2.5 minutes) (AO1 = 2) (50 words maximum)**


In the context of caregiver-infant interactions, reciprocity is a two-way/mutual process; each party responds to the other's signals to sustain interaction through turn-taking. There is interactional synchrony as infant and adult react and respond in time to sustain communication and thus elicit a response from the other.

**(47 words)**


*14 Briefly evaluate research into caregiver-infant interaction.*

**[4 marks] (5 minutes) (AO3 = 4) (100 words maximum)**


There is the possibility of observer bias, as often the researchers are also the main observers. Investigator effects can be nullified however by having two researchers assess the caregiver-infant interaction and by comparing their scores to see if they match or are similar. This is known as inter-rater/observer reliability.

Another issue that researchers might encounter when investigating caregiver-infant interactions is the issue of extraneous variables affecting the results. Well-controlled studies, however, capture micro-sequences of interaction and look to ameliorate the issues of extraneous variables of intentionality in caregiver-infant interaction by discerning if imitative behaviours are deliberate or conscious, for example.

**(100 words)**

*Anca is an orphan who has recently been adopted by a British couple. Before being adopted, Anca lived in an institution with lots of other children in very poor conditions. Her new parents are understandably concerned about how Anca's early experiences may affect her in the future.*

*1 5 Use your knowledge of the effects of institutionalisation to advise Anca's new parents about what to expect.*

**[5 marks] (6.25 minutes) (AO2 = 5) (125 words maximum)**

Institutionalisation can have effects on physical, intellectual, social and emotional development. Anca's parents could be advised to expect that Anca may display signs of Type D 'disinhibited attachment' and Anca may not know how to behave towards strangers.

Another effect could be delayed intellectual development, low IQ problems and difficulty concentrating. Anca may therefore struggle more at school than others in her peer group and may not learn new behaviours and concepts at the same rate.

In terms of her emotional development, Anca may experience more temper tantrums. However, if Anca was adopted before the age of 6 months, the effects may not be as severe and long term as if had she been adopted later. The effects may also be reversed with sensitive parenting.

**(125 words)**

*1 6 Discuss findings of research into cultural variations in attachment.*

**[8 marks] (10 minutes) (AO1 = 3; AO3 = 5) (200 words maximum)**

Van Ijzendoorn and Kroonenberg's research into cultural variations in attachment found that secure attachment was the most common type of attachment in all cultures. Japan and Israel displayed higher levels of insecure-resistant attachment (collectivist cultures) which was supported by Sagi et al (1991) who found high rates of insecure-resistant attachments in Israeli children. Germany (an individualistic culture) showed higher levels of insecure-avoidant attachment. Van Ijzendoorn and Kroonenberg concluded that secure attachment is the type of attachment that is best for healthy development.

(AO1 = 3)

Meta-analyses include very large samples and thus increase the validity of the findings. One issue, however, with Van Ijzendoorn and Kroonenberg's research is that the underlying methodology of the studies in their meta-analysis used the 'strange situation'. They also reported significant differences in the distribution of attachment types in different cultures. For example, Germany had the highest rate of insecure-avoidant attachment which may be the result of different childrearing practices and not a more 'insecure' population. Consequently, the underlying methodology used in their analysis may be biased towards American/British cultures and samples in studies may not represent the culture as a whole. Cultural variations may also be due to an interaction of nature and nurture.

(AO3 = 5)

**(197 words)**

# SECTION D: PSYCHOPATHOLOGY

*Answer <u>all</u> questions in this section (24 marks and 30 minutes for each section on Paper 1)*

*1 7 Which <u>two</u> of the following are cognitive characteristics of obsessive-compulsive disorder (OCD)?*

*Choose <u>two</u> from the options <u>A</u>, <u>B</u>, <u>C</u>, <u>D</u> and <u>E</u>.*

**[2 marks] (2.5 minutes) (AO1 = 2)**

*A Awareness that behaviour is irrational*
*B Compulsions*
*C Disgust*
*D High anxiety*
*E Obsessions*

A
E

*1 8 Outline one or more ways in which behaviourists treat phobias.*

**[6 marks] (7.5 minutes) (AO1 = 6) (150 words maximum)**

Systematic desensitisation is based on classical conditioning and uses counter-conditioning to help patients unlearn their phobias, by eliciting another response; relaxation instead of fear. A patient works with their therapist to create a fear hierarchy, ranking phobic situations from least to most terrifying. After the formation of the anxiety hierarchy, the patient is taught relaxation techniques such as deep breathing. The therapist then gradually works up a patients fear hierarchy until the patient is able to maintain a relaxed state when confronted with the situation that triggers their phobia the most, such as holding a spider if arachnophobic. The patient then no longer associates the stimulus with danger and thus anxiety. Two emotional states (fear and relaxation) cannot coexist at the same time, (a theory known as reciprocal inhibition) and eventually relaxation will replace the fear. Gradual exposure then leads to eventual extinction of the fear of the phobic stimulus.

**(150 words)**

*Rob is a sixth form student who has started hearing voices in his head. The voices come often, are usually threatening and make Rob feel frightened. The voices are making it difficult for Rob to complete his homework properly and he is worried about how this may affect his chances of going to university. Rob has not told anyone about his experiences, but his parents and teachers have noticed that he appears distracted, anxious and untidy.*

*1 9 Outline and evaluate failure to function adequately and deviation from ideal mental health as definitions of abnormality. Refer to the experiences of Rob in your answer.*

**[16 marks] (20 minutes) (AO1 = 6; AO2 = 4; AO3 = 6) (400 words maximum)**

According to the failure to function adequately definition, abnormality is judged as an inability to deal with the demands of everyday living and to live independently in society. A person's behaviour is maladaptive, irrational or dangerous and causes personal distress and distress to others. Rob could be considered abnormal as there is evidence that Rob is not coping with everyday tasks, finding it difficult to 'complete his homework' and he is 'untidy'. Rob has personal distress i.e.; feelings of anxiety and he is 'frightened' and his symptoms are also causing distress as 'his parents and teachers' have noticed his anxiety.

(AO1 = 3; AO2 = 2)

The failure to function adequately definition recognises the patient's perspective and judging a person, in this case, Rob, as distressed or distressing relies on subjective assessment. It is therefore, a useful tool for assessing psychopathological behaviour. However, not all abnormal behaviour is associated with distress and a failure to cope i.e., psychopathy, and not all maladaptive behaviour is an indicator of mental illness. There is also the issue of individual differences, for example, one person who hears voices may be unable to function adequately; whereas, another person may suffer from the same symptoms, but function; thus, questioning the validity of this definition.

(AO3 = 3)

Deviation from ideal mental health is another definition of abnormality whereby the absence of signs of mental health is used to judge abnormality. Jahoda (1958) outlined a series of principles, including: accurate perception of reality, resistance to stress; positive attitude towards self; autonomy/independence; environmental mastery and self–actualisation. It could be argued that Rob does not have an accurate view of reality as he is 'hearing voices'. The voices are also potentially preventing Rob from fulfilling his potential and achieving self–actualisation and 'may affect his chances of going to university.' According to this definition, the more criteria someone fails to meet, the more abnormal they are.

(AO1 = 3; AO2 = 2)

Jahoda's definition takes a positive, holistic approach to diagnosis.  However, the criteria for mental health are arguably too demanding and unrealistic. There is some correlation with deviation from social norms as a definition of abnormality which outlines an individual who contrasts with the behaviours of their society (the social norms) and deviation from statistical norms which is behaviour that is rare statistically and is considered abnormal. There is cultural bias also in some of Jahoda's criteria, i.e., the value placed on independence and autonomy could be considered to be culturally relative and biased.

(AO3 = 3)

**(400 words)**

# ASSESSMENT OBJECTIVES.

There are three assessment objectives assessed in each examination: **AO1, AO2** and **AO3.**

**AO1 = Outline.** This involves outlining your knowledge and understanding. It involves recalling and describing theories, studies and methods.

**AO2 = Apply.** This involves applying your knowledge and understanding. You must apply your knowledge to different situations and contexts. You will apply this from the information given in the text provided in the question; which will be a theoretical or practical example.

**AO3 = Evaluate.** This involves analysing and interpreting.
Evaluating studies and theories or drawing conclusions.

There may be one, two or all (only in the extended writing questions) of the assessment objectives in each question. Therefore, it is vitally important to be aware of the structure of how the assessment objectives are allocated in each question of the exam in order to maximise your opportunities to obtain full marks in each question.

It is worth noting that **the Assessment Objectives that are to be met for each question are not provided in the examination itself**, which provides a further complication for you. However, I have provided which assessment objectives are being assessed in the practice questions in this book to give you more awareness of what each type of question is looking for in the answer.

<u>Additional points to remember.</u>

1) When you are answering the AO2 application section of the question, write 'In terms of application' before providing your AO2 points and give a quotation if possible, particularly if the question is asking you to 'refer' back to the information provided. Also, when you are answering the AO3 evaluation section of the question, write 'In terms of evaluation' before providing your AO3 points.

2) Generally, my students prefer to separate the AO's out in their answers i.e., for a 12 mark (AO1 = 6; AO3 =6) answer they will write 2 paragraphs with the first paragraph being AO1 (6 marks) and then the second paragraph being AO3 (6 marks) or 4 paragraphs with 3 marks of AO1 or A03 in each paragraph.

# TIMINGS.

Please allocate minutes per mark! In the Psychology AQA A level examination papers there are 96 marks to aim for in 120 minutes; which works out at **1.25 minutes per mark**. (This is the same minutes per mark as in all your AS and A level Papers). Therefore, **if a question is worth 8 marks then you would spend roughly 10 minutes** on this question. In the examples in this book, I have given you the maximum amount of time allowed for each question which always works out at **1.25 minutes per mark.**

A good rule of thumb is to apply the principle that you get **1 mark per correct point made in your answer** i.e., 4 good points for a 4-mark question. My students find that writing 1 sentence per mark also helps them to apply this rule generally. Similar to all the principles in this book, **you must apply and follow the correct timings for each question and stick to them throughout your exam to get an A or A star in your Psychology examinations.**

If you have extra time allocated to you, just change the calculation to accommodate the extra time you have for each mark i.e., approximately 1.5 minutes per mark if you have 25% extra time and approximately 1.8 minutes per mark if you have 50% extra time. Allocate within your time management the time for checking if you wish but **move on from the set question as soon as you have reached or are coming towards your time limit**. This ensures that you have excellent coverage of your whole exam and therefore attain a very good mark.

Without applying this principle in these examinations (and to a large extent all examinations) you cannot achieve the highest marks! **Apply all of the principles provided in this book to succeed!**

Additional points to remember.

1) **10% of your examination will be composed of mathematical questions**. But please do not be overly concerned, it is only GCSE level Mathematics and involves basic arithmetic, data and graphs.

2) **Approximately a third of all questions at AS and A level Psychology will involve Research Methods** and they can occur in any paper or section of your examinations, not just in the Research Methods section. **Please make sure you apply a strong focus to Research Methods in your revision** and remember again that the Mathematics involved is only set at a GCSE level of difficulty.

# APPROXIMATE WORD COUNT PER MARK IN PSYCHOLOGY.

Now that you know what is on each examination, how the assessment objectives are assessed and the time allocated for each type of question we come to what would be considered the correct word count per mark for each question. The primary principle though is to spend the right amount of time on each question as mentioned on the previous pages.

Unfortunately, there is no exact rule here as some questions are mathematical and do not require words whilst extended writing questions and essays tend to follow the set word count below more exactly.

In the answers in this book, I have provided the maximum word count for each answer which works out at **25 words per mark**. However, a good rule of thumb is between **15 and 25 words**.

15 words per mark – minimum word count.

20 words per mark – a generally good word count per mark.

25 words per mark – **The maximum word count generally able to be produced, in the time allocated.**

<u>Additional points to remember.</u>

1) If your answer has quality, 25 words per mark gives you the best chance of obtaining the highest marks in your Psychology exam. Obviously, it does not if you are waffling however. (Please remember to answer the question set and to move on in the time allocated.)

2) Generally, Research Methods questions tend to need less words per mark but there are exceptions to this rule.

3) Remember: **Apply the principle that you get 1 mark per correct point made in your answer and 1 sentence per mark also helps to apply this rule** and if you are concise you can obtain each mark in 15 words of writing. I am aware that some students can write faster than others but all should be able to write 15 words per mark at A level in 1.25 minutes (if they have not been allocated extra time). This is where conciseness is important. However, using the principle of one point per sentence: **Each point/sentence and therefore mark should generally be between 15 and 25 words and completed in 1.25 minutes.**

4) My students have applied all the techniques I am providing you with to gain A's and A stars in their Psychology examinations. You can replicate them by following the advice in this book.

Very best wishes for your examinations!

Thank you for purchasing this book,

Joseph

Printed in Great Britain
by Amazon